IMAGES OF SCOTLAND

MIDLOTHIAN

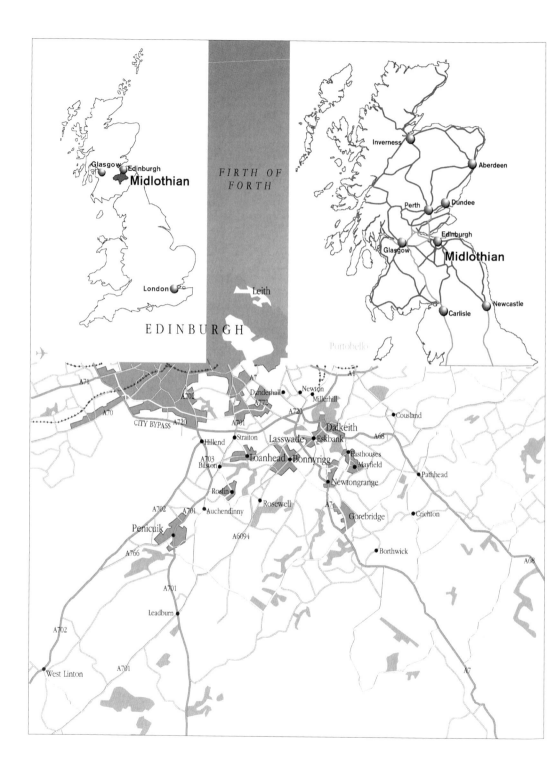

IMAGES OF SCOTLAND

MIDLOTHIAN

KENNETH R. BOGLE

TEMPUS

First published 2006

Tempus Publishing Limited
The Mill, Brimscombe Port,
Stroud, Gloucestershire, GL5 2QG
www.tempus-publishing.com

British Library Cataloguing in Publication Data.
A catalogue record for this book is available from the British Library.

ISBN 0 7524 4066 7

Typesetting and origination by Tempus Publishing Limited.
Printed in Great Britain.

Contents

Acknowledgements

One of the pleasures of compiling this book has been to meet people whose knowledge of their local area is, and always will be, vastly superior to my own. Amongst the many local people who helped me, I would particularly like to thank David Adams, Norman Brett, Bill Bruce and the Penicuik Historical Society, Alex McKinnon, Marion Richardson, Alex Smith, David Smith, Craig Statham and Winnie Stevenson.

The photographs in this book are taken from the collections of Midlothian Local Studies, where I am currently employed. I am grateful to my work colleagues for their encouragement and support. I would particularly like to thank Sylvia Blyth, Neil MacVicar and Katherine Morgan. Scott Ballantye kindly supplied the map. Thanks are also due to Philip Wark and Alan Reid, managers of a superior ilk who agreed to support the project.

I would like to thank the many people who have donated photographs to Midlothian Local Studies over the years. Thanks also to my wife Alison, travelling companion around Midlothian.

Finally, I would like to thank everyone at Tempus Publishing for their imagination and encouragement, especially to my editor David Buxton.

I need hardly add that what follows is my own work and that any errors are my own. The good people mentioned here are entirely blameless and I apologise for my own fallibility.

I have made every effort to trace the holders of copyright material and apologise if I have inadvertently infringed copyright.

Introduction

Lying to the south of Edinburgh and occupying the valley between the Pentland and Moorfoot hills, Midlothian is an area of rich agricultural land, industrial developments and dynamic local communities. The population of around 80,000 people is mainly concentrated in the north of the district and is renowned for its friendliness, strength and resilience.

The character and prosperity of Midlothian have always been closely linked to Edinburgh. Indeed for much of its life Midlothian was known as 'Edinburghshire'. Edinburgh has long made use of Midlothian for essential supplies, such as water, food and coal, and also for recreation and leisure. In return, the people of Midlothian have exploited the wide range of services and opportunities that the city has to offer. The main transport routes through Midlothian spread out from Edinburgh, and even today it is often easier to travel between town and city than it is to travel from town to town. Before local government reorganisation in 1975, the county of Midlothian extended from West Calder in the west, down to Stow in the south and round to Musselburgh in the east: roughly speaking, a horseshoe of land encircling Edinburgh. The County Buildings were not even in Midlothian at this time, but in Edinburgh, emphasising the county's dependency on the city. In 1975, the county area was considerably reduced and local government headquarters were established in Dalkeith. Since then, Midlothian's identity has become increasingly focused on its own area.

There has long been an exodus from Edinburgh into Midlothian. Wealthy people and others have moved to enjoy the greater freedoms of the surrounding countryside. For example, the Clerks of Penicuik, a talented and versatile family, bought land near Penicuik. Sir James Clerk, the 3rd baronet, built Penicuik House to his own design from 1761. Artists and writers have also settled in Midlothian, such as the novelist Sir Walter Scott and the painter William McTaggart. This book contains several photographs taken by the Steuarts of Mount Esk, a wealthy legal family from Edinburgh who had a summer home near Lasswade. More recently, incomers from the city have taken advantage of various new housing schemes.

Midlothian has a long and fascinating history. Early peoples left their imprint on the local landscape, such as the hill-fort and souterrain at Castlelaw in the Pentland hills, which dates from the first - second century CE. The Romans marched into Scotland along the line of what is now the A68, leaving behind a series of forts and earthworks, such as Elginhaugh near Dalkeith. In the Middle Ages, Midlothian often bore the brunt of the endemic warfare between Scotland and England. In 1303, a Scottish army inflicted a substantial defeat on an English force at the Battle of Roslin. In the twelfth century, King Malcolm IV founded the Augustinian hospital at Soutra in the lonely Moorfoot hills to serve travellers on the traditional route into England. During the Civil War, soldiers under Cromwell used St Nicholas parish church in Dalkeith and Roslin chapel as barracks and stables. They also destroyed Roslin Castle and bombarded Borthwick Castle. In 1666, an army of Covenanters, opponents of episcopacy in church government in Scotland, was defeated at Rullion Green in the Pentlands, just above Penicuik. In more peaceful times, great families developed mansion houses and pleasure grounds, such as Melville Castle, Newbattle Abbey and Dalhousie Castle. In the nineteenth century, Midlothian shared fully in the profound changes in Scottish life and society, the result of which can be seen in places such as Newtongrange and Rosewell. Like other parts of Britain, local industries, such as papermaking and coal mining, have risen and declined as fashions and economics have dictated.

This book is intended to give a general portrait of Midlothian and to capture some of its history and culture. The photographs in the book are taken from the collection of Midlothian Local Studies, currently housed in Loanhead and part of Midlothian Council Library Service. The collection has been built up over the years, partly by purchase but largely by donation from generous locals. The collection includes many rare prints, postcards, slides and glass plate negatives. The photographs in this book represent some of the best images from the collection, but for every one that I have included several others have been left out due to lack of space. I have tried to use photographs that have not been previously published, although I have included a handful that might be familiar but are worthy of inclusion because they are such striking images and illustrate a particular theme. I have concentrated on the period between 1890 to 1930 with a few later photographs as well. This period was something of a heyday for amateur photography as the costs of equipment and processing began to fall and photography became more accessible. Many of the photographs in this book are the work of dedicated amateur enthusiasts, such as the Bryce family of Roslin or the Black family of Penicuik, which were subsequently donated to Midlothian Local Studies. I have also used picture postcards, which were produced in huge quantities in the Edwardian era, often covering the minutiae of local life. The photographs have been chosen on individual merit, although I have included a few images of slightly lesser quality because of their historic significance.

The book is divided into six chapters. Chapter one is a photographic Tour of Midlothian, showing many places of interest in the area. Chapter two looks at the People of Midlothian, starting at the higher end of the social scale and working down. Chapter three examines Working Lives; Chapter four, Travel and Transport; Chapter five, Sport and Leisure; and Chapter six, Days to Remember, a miscellany of memorable events and occasions.

I greatly enjoyed compiling this book and I hope that other people, natives and non-natives, will like it too. Midlothian is an interesting and beautiful place. It is worth getting to know.

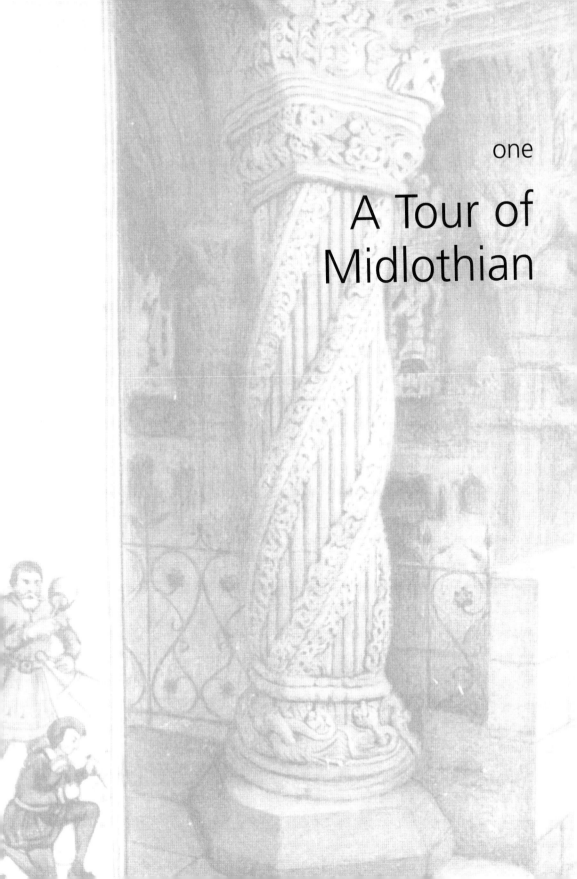

one

A Tour of
Midlothian

Above: The Pentland hills are not very rugged or high, but they are a well-loved feature of the Midlothian landscape. The Pentlands offer beautiful scenery, natural wilderness, history and solitude, and have inspired many of Scotland's greatest writers and artists. This photograph shows the valley of the Logan Burn and Loganlee Reservoir in the heart of the northern hills.

Left: On the southern side of the Pentland hills, Nine Mile Burn is nine miles from Edinburgh. It was the site of a famous coaching inn and smithy, which is remembered in Alexander Rodger's song 'Robin Tamson's Smiddy'. The thatched building shown in this postcard was demolished about 1910. George Meikle Kemp, the architect of the Scott Monument in Princes Street Gardens, Edinburgh, was brought up in the vicinity.

ALLAN RAMSAY'S MONUMENT, PENTLANDS

This obelisk at Ravensneuk near Penicuik was erected in 1759 to commemorate Allan Ramsay (1684-1758). A successful and popular poet, Ramsay was friendly with the Forbes family of Newhall, near Carlops. The house is the setting of his greatest work, the pastoral comedy *The Gentle Shepherd*, which describes rustic life and courtship amongst the Pentland hills.

Ancestral home of the Clerk family, Penicuik House was built between 1761-1778 and represented the ideal of a Scots Palladian house set in a romantic landscape. The house was gutted by fire in 1899, although most of the furniture and fittings were saved, as shown in this picture taken the morning after the fire. The family then moved to the converted stable block nearby.

The origins of modern Penicuik can be traced back to about 1770 when Sir James Clerk of Penicuik planned and laid out part of the new village. This photograph from 1902 shows the spacious High Street looking west, possibly taken during the coronation of Edward VII.

Penicuik High Street looking in the opposite direction, pictured in 1915. The town grew rich on papermaking. The mill-owning Cowan family was very influential and built the Cowan Institute, in the centre of the picture, in 1893. St Mungo's, the sturdy parish church of 1771, is at the end of the street.

The pleasant little village of Auchendinny, shown here in 1904, occupies a steeply sloping riverbank site on the Glencorse burn. Just south of the village, Auchendinny house was the home of Henry Mackenzie (1745-1831), essayist and author of the novel *The Man of Feeling*.

Milton Bridge sits on the main Edinburgh-Penicuik highway, but there was only one horse-drawn cart on the road when this picture was taken in 1904.

Above: Glencorse old church has been a religious site for many centuries and featured in several works by Robert Louis Stevenson. This early photograph shows the church before it fell into disrepair in the 1880s. The man in the photograph is Alexander Torrence, who was minister for almost forty years. The old church was restored in 2002.

Left: Dryden Tower, an eye-catching nineteenth-century folly near Loanhead, is a remnant of the Dryden estate. The handsome baronial estate house, originally constructed by the Lockhart family, was demolished in 1938.

Opposite: The landscaped grounds of the Dryden estate included this beautiful avenue of beech trees.

Above: Hawthornden Castle is dramatically situated high above the River North Esk, near Roslin. It was the home of William Drummond (1585-1649), the celebrated poet and historian. A complex range of buildings, there is also an extraordinary and mysterious warren of caves carved into the rock beneath the castle.

Above: The collegiate church of St Matthew, otherwise known as Rosslyn chapel, is unquestionably the most important and enigmatic building in Midlothian. Founded in 1446 by William St Clair, the third Prince of Orkney, the interior is rich with elaborate carvings of vegetation and religious and secular figures. Recently, the building has been featured in the best-selling novel *The Da Vinci Code.*

Right: The best-known story about Rosslyn chapel is that of the Apprentice Pillar. It is said that an apprentice mason carved an elaborate column and his master was so envious at the quality of the work that he killed the apprentice on the spot.

Opposite below: Midlothian has some areas of outstanding natural beauty, in particular Roslin Glen, where the River North Esk winds through a spectacular steep-sided gorge. Once the site of a large gunpowder mill, the Glen has long been a favourite place for picnics and riverside walks.

THE PRENTICE PILLAR ROSLIN CHAPEL. FOUNDED 1446 BY WILLIAM St Clair. R P Phillimore

Above: The compact village of Roswell was built by the Lothian Coal Company to house miners employed at the nearby Whitehill pit. The village was once known as 'Little Ireland' because of the large number of Irish immigrants. This postcard shows the local post office. A poster on the wall says: 'Do you play football? Then join the Royal Scots'.

Above: Loanhead has a long history as a working town, especially in coal mining. This postcard shows the High Street looking east, *c.* 1910. With the exception of the building on the left (now the post office), everything else in this picture has been demolished.

Right: Built between 1786 and 1791 on the site of a medieval hunting lodge, Melville Castle was designed by James Playfair for Henry Dundas, the first Viscount Melville. The building has three storeys with round windowed corner turrets and two-storey wings. It is now a luxury hotel.

Opposite below: Photographed around 1910, Polton is a tiny village on the River North Esk and once had two paper mills and a railway station, shown here on the left. In 1840, the author and notorious opium addict Thomas De Quincey (1785-1859) took up residence at Mavisbush Cottage in Polton.

A panoramic view of Lasswade village looking across to the parish church, which was demolished in 1956. The old village of Lasswade was built on the steep slopes of the North Esk valley at an important crossing point over the river.

Sir Walter Scott (1771–1832) had many associations with Midlothian and there are many references to the area in his work. Following his marriage in 1797, Scott rented Barony or Lasswade Cottage, as it was then known, from the Clerks of Penicuik. It became a centre of literary activity and Scott received many important guests whilst living there.

The Cross Roads. Bonnyrigg.

Bonnyrigg became a burgh in 1865 and amalgamated with its neighbour Lasswade in 1929. The Commercial Bank building was erected about 1925. Across the road was George Dick's Boot and Shoe warehouse.

COCKPEN CHURCH, BONNYRIGG.

The ruined Cockpen old parish church is the earliest church in Midlothian. It holds the seventeenth-century Dalhousie vaults and many interesting gravestones. The new parish church was built between 1818 and 1820, and holds the bell from the earlier building.

Dalkeith High Street, looking east, *c.* 1900. The town was a thriving market and agricultural centre, and also had many small trades and manufactures, such as brewing and an iron foundry.

Opposite above: Bounded by the North and South Esk, Dalkeith is the county town of Midlothian with a history that can be traced back to the Middle Ages. In this photograph from around 1900, the spire of St Nicholas parish church dominates the skyline. Parts of the church date from the fifteenth century.

Right: Until regeneration after the Second World War, Dalkeith was a maze of narrow closes. This photograph shows Vint's Close, named after William Vint, merchant and shipmaster, *c.* 1900. The mud-filled cobbled road and closely packed buildings encouraged the spread of infectious diseases.

Below: At one time the principal home of the Buccleuch family, Dalkeith House is one of Scotland's great classical houses. Originally a twelfth-century castle, it was reconstructed in the early eighteenth century for Anne, Duchess of Buccleuch. The house has extensive grounds, including an ornate, twelve-sided conservatory, built in 1832-4, now sadly derelict. (Courtesy of Michael Bannister)

Newbattle Abbey was founded in 1140 and became one of the great monastic houses of medieval Scotland. Parts of the earlier building were incorporated into the later mansion house, a seat of the Marquis of Lothian. In 1936 it became an adult education centre.

Newbattle Abbey is set in a beautiful country estate and has formal Italian gardens at the rear of the house. The famous beech tree was estimated to have been 400 years old and grew to 105 feet in height and measured 43 feet round the base. Seven drooping branches rooted in the ground around it. The tree fell in a gale on 15 January 1952.

The red sandstone castle of Dalhousie dates from the fifteenth century, although it has had many transformations and additions. The former seat of the Ramsays, who converted the castle into a fine renaissance house, it was used as a school from 1925 to 1950 and then converted into a hotel.

Main Street, Newtongrange, c. 1900. The brick building on the left was the original Dean Tavern, which was opened in 1899 by the village owners, the Lothian Coal Company. The Dean was a 'Gothenburg' public house based on a Swedish system where drinking was controlled and profits were put back into the community. The old building was notoriously cold and was replaced in 1910. (Courtesy of Alex Smith)

Bare-footed children play in Gorebridge High Street, which is free of traffic, *c.* 1900. Gorebridge once had a thriving gunpowder manufactory (Stobs Mill 1794-1875), which was superseded by coal mining.

Begun in 1726, Arniston House near Gorebridge took over thirty years to build. The home of the Dundas family, it was designed by William Adam, but completed by his son John. The house and surrounding estate is still owned by the Dundas family.

The massive six-storey Borthwick Castle dates from the fifteenth century, although it was restored in the 1890s after many years of dereliction. Borthwick parish church dates from the 1860s, but it contains traces of its twelfth-century predecessor, including the tomb of the first Lord Borthwick (*c.* 1470).

South of Gorebridge, the hamlet of Fushie Bridge was once the first staging post on the road from Edinburgh to Carlisle. In 1846, there was a serious riot between Scottish workmen and Irish navvies. Most of the village was demolished in the 1960s because of substandard houses.

Cousland has had a working smiddy since 1703. The village smiddy played a vital role in the local community. Horses needed shoes and carriages and other items had to be repaired. This postcard shows the brick chimney and pantiled roof. Villagers recently formed a working trust to preserve the building.

Built around a sixteenth-century tower, Oxenfoord Castle, the seat of the Dalrymple family, was enlarged by Robert Adam in 1782 and modernised by William Burn in the 1840s. Sir John Dalrymple wrote the influential *An Essay on Landscape Gardening* in 1774. At one time a school for girls, the castle is now available for weddings and other events.

A typical rural village, Pathhead is a long ribbon of houses divided by a wide main street. There is evidence of a Roman temporary camp in fields at the top of the village.

The tiny village of Fala nestles on the northern foothills of the Lammermuirs. The A68 road runs close by, but still leaves the village pleasantly isolated. When this photograph was taken around 1915 it was clearly a big event for local boys.

Shown in this postcard from 1907, Carrington is a peaceful and charming village of single-storey pantiled cottages. Carrington has also been known as Primrose because of connections with the earls of Rosebery.

The quiet and remote village of Temple in the south of Midlothian was once the Scottish headquarters of the Knights Templar. The roofless old parish church dates from the early fourteenth century and is the only surviving Templar building in Scotland. The churchyard contains a number of interesting headstones.

two

The People of MIdlothian

The Steuarts of Mount Esk were a wealthy legal family. Their house stood on an escarpment of the River North Esk near Lasswade and was used as a summer retreat from Edinburgh. A collection of glass plate negatives belonging to the Steuarts was rediscovered in the 1980s. They provide a vivid insight into the lives of an upper middle class family living in Midlothian at the end of the nineteenth century. Above: three generations of the Steuart family: Archibald, his son James and granddaughter Sylvia.

Belles of the ball. Christian and Janet Steuart, daughters of Archibald. Christian took a keen interest in village life, where she was known as 'Miss Steuart'. She never married and died in Edinburgh in 1957. Note the narrow waistlines, which were fashionable at the time.

Right: This snaggle-toothed old lady is thought to be Catherine Steuart, the spinster sister of Archibald. Aunt Kate spent most of her life at Mount Esk looking after her father and brother until her death in 1890.

Below: The Victorians are often thought of as being very stiff and formal, but there were many light-hearted moments and genuine affection. This loving couple are thought to be Thomas Steuart and Georgina Bell, better known as Uncle Tote and Aunt Dodi. The couple lived in Edinburgh, but had a summer residence, Stellknowe, close to the railway station at Leadburn.

More photographs from the Steuart family album. Christian, in her gardening gloves, George and a female friend enjoy a summer afternoon in the garden. Hats and parasols were essential for a stroll around the garden.

Fashion for women. Maria Steuart was a cousin of the Steuarts of Mount Esk. She is wearing a handsome checked dress with a typical narrow waistline and a matching hat. The elderly gentleman and dog have not been identified.

Right: Fashion for men. James Steuart and possibly one of his uncles. Informal dress was largely unknown and both of these men are wearing stiffly starched collars and ties or cravats. As well as the striking check jacket, George's companion is wearing spats and a bowler hat. George sports slip-on shoes, which seem quite modern.

Below: Fashion for children. Sailor suits remained popular for children into the 1920s.

Annie S. Swan was born in 1859 near
Coldingham in the Scottish Borders, the
daughter of a farmer. She spent much of
her early life in Edinburgh and Gorebridge,
where she wrote her first successful novel
Aldersyde (1883) and married James Burnett
Smith, a local schoolteacher. A shrewd,
energetic and humorous woman, she was
a prolific and immensely popular author
who wrote over 150 books and journalism,
including a magazine under her own name.

Samuel Rutherford Crockett (1859-1914)
was appointed minister to the Free Church
in Penicuik in 1886. S.R. Crockett combined
his religious duties with a literary career and
was a leading writer of historical adventure
stories and journalism. His novels were
hugely successful and he later resigned his
post and devoted himself full-time to writing.

Right: Andrew Dodds (1872-1959), pictured here with his wife Annie and Jessie Young, was a popular Midlothian poet who wrote about rural themes, often in the local dialect. A draper to trade, he lived in Easthouses, Pathhead and Dalkeith, and was an active socialist, particularly in slum clearance and for the rights of farm workers. Dodds was a great humanitarian and during the First World War he served with the YMCA in France.

Below: William McTaggart (1835-1910) is widely regarded as Scotland's greatest landscape painter. Born near Campbeltown to Gaelic-speaking parents, his oil paintings developed a freedom of expression and technique that was highly original for the time. McTaggart spent the last twenty years of his life at Dean Park House, Broomieknowe, where he lived with his second wife Marjory and their children. This photograph shows him at work in his studio at Dean Park.

Walter Girdwood McNab opened a chemist shop on Main Street, Gorebridge in 1894. As well as prescriptions, he sold his own remedies, including a brand of cough mixture called 'Cough Easier'. His remedies always included instructions to 'shake the bottle', earning him the nickname 'Auld Shake the Bottle'. McNab was also a skilled photographer and many of his photographs were sold locally as postcards.

Archibald Hood (1823-1902) was one of the most remarkable men in nineteenth-century mining. From humble origins in Kilmarnock, he became Managing Director of the Midlothian Coal Company and the Glamorgan Coal Company in South Wales. A determined and energetic man, he was a brilliant engineer who took a great paternal interest in the welfare of his workers, building schools, libraries and decent houses.

Above: Penicuik South Church Choir photographed in 1903. Back row: R. Jack, R. Black, James Bell, Bobby Young, Mr Douglas, Jim Cockburn, Mr Taylor, Danny Holt, Jim Wallace, Mr Ritchie, Jim Breslim, Bob Mitchell and Dick Rutherford. Middle row: Rae Mitchell, Mae Steel, J. Harvey, Mrs Dunlop, Mary Mason, Jean Steel, Mr Chisholm, A Mitchell, Miss Craster, Mrs Robb, Lizzie Blair, Mrs Fotheringham and Miss Campbell. Front row: Dolly Nisison, Miss Cockburn, Annie Milne and Nellie Anderson.

Right: The Porteous sisters, Bella and Ina, ran the post office in Loanhead around the time of the First World War.

The Bryce family were well-known residents of Roslin. George and Fanny Bryce ran the local drapers and post office, which was passed on to their daughters Marion and Margaret (standing middle and right). Margaret's husband Tom Ritchie was a keen amateur photographer and some of his photographs appear in this book.

The Young family of Roslin, photographed during the First World War. Back row: Bessie, Ann, George, Helen and Margaret. Front row: Margaret and David. The Young family ran the Craigathrie tea rooms in Roslin, which was a favourite stopping place for visitors to the village.

Two working
men from the
Newtongrange
area, *c.* 1930. The
cloth cap was a
badge of class
identity.

This cheerful group of musicians with two mandolins, fiddle and accordion was photographed outside Edmonstone village hall in the 1920s. The mandolin was an unusual instrument in Midlothian, which might have been introduced by immigrants from Eastern Europe who were brought in to work in mines belonging to the Midlothian Coal Company.

Photographed in the 1930s, Mrs Briggs and her dogs stand outside her home at 21 Main Street, Newtongrange. The house was rented from the Lothian Coal Company, like hundreds of others in the area.

Bairns. Three unidentified girls from Newtongrange, *c.* 1910.

A gang of boys pose for the camera at Thorburn Terrace, Penicuik. (Courtesy of Penicuik Historical Society)

Charlie Smith, seated here on a pony with a dummy rifle, was a well-known character in Penicuik.

James 'Deak' Thomson (1821-1898) was a famous Midlothian character. A cattle dealer, he lost all his money in a bad business deal and thereafter grew increasingly eccentric. He refused to stay in the Penicuik poorhouse, preferring to live in extreme poverty in his own house at Silverburn. He loved hill running at local sports days, although organising committees would pay him not to take part as 'his costume was scarcely up to date as regards repair'.

The birdman of Penicuik. This unidentified man clearly had a close affinity with owls. (Courtesy of Penicuik Historical Society)

Alexander 'Eckie' Petrie was a celebrated Penicuik worthy. A general labourer, he was known as the 'Bank Street Boy' and was the butt of many jokes.

A native of County Mayo, Johnny Toole was Penicuik town crier and bellman. He was also a travelling comedian, musician and step-dancer who performed throughout the country. He was best known as a ringmaster or 'Merry Andrew' at country fairs and sports, where he would entertain the crowds, often dressed in his colourful costume.

Philip and Jean were familiar figures in the parish of Dalkeith who earned a meagre living by selling laces and ribbons from a basket. When Philip had been drinking, Jean would remove his stick until he was fit to walk by himself. They spent much of their time sitting at the roadside watching the world go past.

GERMAN GIPSIES. MCNAB.

A postcard of gypsies in Gorebridge in 1906. They were variously described as 'German', 'Serbian' or 'Croatian'. Several families of gypsies were regular visitors to the Midlothian area, setting up temporary camps outside local communities and sometimes giving performances of songs. With their exotic Romany look, they were obvious outsiders and on one occasion a group was arrested as spies.

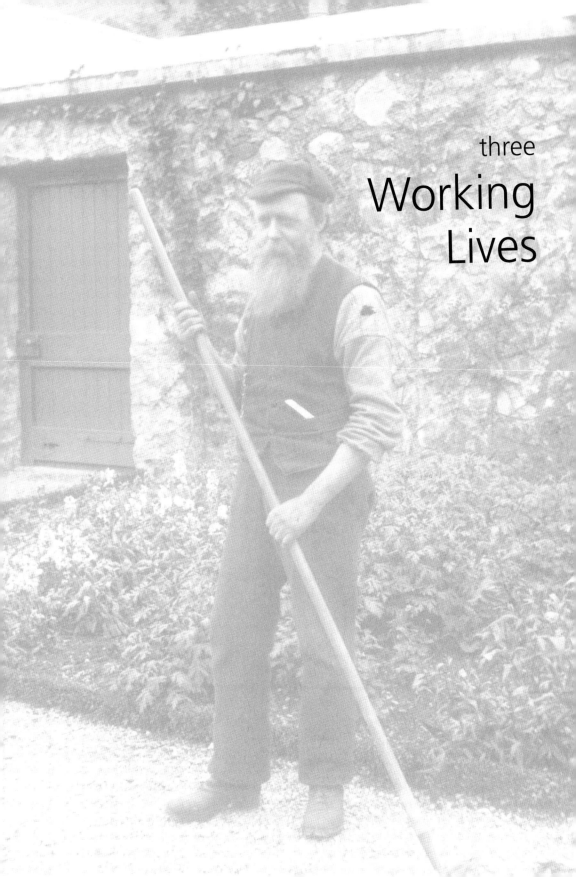

three
Working
Lives

GENERAL VIEW, NEWTONGRANGE.

Coal mining was the most distinctive of all Midlothian industries. It can be traced back to the thirteenth century when the monks of Newbattle Abbey supervised the winning of coal or 'black stanis' from outcrops or drift mines. In the nineteenth century, the vast deposits of deeper-lying coal became accessible thanks to the new technology of steam-power and the railway system. This in turn led to the creation of planned communities such as Newtongrange and Rosewell, and the enlargement of older villages such as Gorebridge and Newton. This postcard from the late 1930s shows a street scene in Newtongrange with miners' housing on the right and shops and the cinema on the left.

Photographed here in July 1898, the Jack pit at Vogrie, near Gorebridge, was operated by the Arniston Coal Company. The shaft of the pit was 63 fathoms deep (around 380 feet).

The Lady Victoria pit at Newtongrange was the centrepiece of the Midlothian coal industry. Owned by the newly formed Lothian Coal Company, sinking began in August 1890 and the pit was opened five years later.

LADY VICTORIA PIT BOTTOM, NEWTONGRANGE.

'The Lady' at Newtongrange was one of the deepest mines in the country, the shaft extending 1,624 feet. It was the first shaft in Scotland to be sunk and walled simultaneously. The underground main roads at the Lady Victoria were substantially built and were illuminated by electricity. Ponies were originally used for hauling.

SCENE AT COAL FACE, LADY VICTORIA PIT, NEWTONGRANGE.

This remarkable postcard shows the coal face, visible in the centre right. The face was only a few feet high and held up with wooden props. The chalk markings on the wooden 'hutch' are probably contractor's marks, indicating ownership of the coal.

The manufacture of gunpowder in Midlothian started at Gorebridge in 1794. Shortly afterwards, Messrs Hay and Merrick set up a factory in Roslin Glen, which continued until the 1950s. Taken around 1905, these workers are wearing woollen protective clothing to prevent the risk of explosions. Jackets and trousers had bone buttons, no pockets and no metal of any kind.

Andrew Fuller Hargreaves was consulting chemist at Roslin gunpowder mills and later became manager. A distinguished chemist, he is shown here at work in the laboratory. He carried out many experiments during his working life to improve the manufacture of gunpowder.

Midlothian has some rich agricultural land and farming was a traditional way of life. Taken around 1910, this photograph shows haymaking at Slatebarns Farm, near Roslin. Ideally, 'winning the hay' took place in early autumn when the weather was dry. The big stacks or 'sows' were built, thatched to keep the rain out, and each was topped with a symbol to show which farm it belonged to.

'Kyling the hay' at Swanston in the Pentland hills, c. 1920. The farmer and his boy with a Clydesdale horse are gathering the hay into 'stooks' to allow it to dry. In the background are the scree-eroded slopes of Allermuir Hill.

This photograph shows a group of bondagers at Hilltown Farm at Newton. Bondagers were women farmworkers, hired to labour in the fields. They were a very important part of the rural labour force in South-East Scotland. Two of the women are wearing the traditional bonnets called 'uglies' to keep the weather off their faces and preserve their complexions.

Fallhills, "The Clipping Time," Penicuik.

Shearing the sheep of their winter coats was an important annual task for farmers and usually involved workers from neighbouring farms. In this postcard, the farmer, William Graham is in the centre with the stick. His wife is standing in the centre with other workers. Two collie dogs are waiting to round up any stragglers.

Above: Many of the large estate houses of Midlothian had huge formal gardens, which required constant maintenance. Taken around 1914, this photograph shows the gardening staff at Mavisbank House, near Loanhead, holding the tools of their trade. Originally built for the Clerk family of Penicuik, at this time the house was used as a private psychiatric hospital called New Saughton Hall.

Left: Miss M.E. Burton was the head gardener at Mavisbank and is shown here in the tomato greenhouse.

Above: Taken from an album of 1900 by Robert Craig, a visitor from Dunbar, this photograph shows a gardener pruning a long length of trained plants at either Lugton or Dalkeith House, where there were beautiful gardens. This may have been a laburnum or rose walk.

Right: One of the gardeners at Mount Esk, the home of the Steuart family.

Midlothian has been associated with papermaking since the late seventeenth century. The River Esk provided process water and was a source of driving machinery, and there an insatiable demand for paper from the publishing houses in Edinburgh. This is Cowan's paper mill in Valleyfield, Penicuik in 1937, the largest of the Midlothian paper mills.

Ragpickers at Valleyfield Mill, *c.* 1905. Every paper mill had rag house where rags were sorted, cut and cleaned before they could be processed to make paper. The work was dirty and unhealthy because of the dust in the air. Here, the women workers wear scarves and aprons but they have no protective facemasks.

A worker tends a papermaking machine at Valleyfield Mill, 1937. This is the dry end of the processing. Paper was fed onto the large rollers at the front of the picture, which were lifted off the machine and stored.

Workers and a cutting machine at Valleyfield in 1909.

Postal and communications workers were a vital part of the local economy, employing everybody from telegram boys to counter clerks. This photograph from 1912 shows the staff of Penicuik post office. The stripes on the front of the elderly man's jacket indicate his length of service.

The post office in John Street, Penicuik with workers Miss Annie Dickie, Miss Forsyth and John Milne, photographed in 1904.

Workers at P&D Lyle's print works at Dalkeith. Lyle's produced a range of finished articles, such as newspapers, booklets and tickets as well as postcards.

Workers, including two women, at the Whitehill Colliery Brick and Fireclay works, *c*. 1930. Most of the workers lived in nearby Rosewell village.

Staff at Hugh Kerr's bakery, Loanhead, *c.* 1905. Situated on the corner of Clerk Street and Church Street, the shop was famous for its currant loaves.

CATCUNE MILLS FUSHIEBRIDGE

Dalkeith was once the biggest grain market in Scotland. A few miles to the south, Catcune grain mills produced barley, oatmeal, pease-meal and brosemeal. After milling, the finished products were shipped all over the world. The mill had a long and eventful history, having been twice badly damaged by fire. It finally closed in 1979.

A Midlothian County Council steam lorry, a Sentinel, which was used to carry rocks for road building and other construction work, in the early 1930s.

House builders at work on the Penicuik Road, Roslin. One hundred years on, the houses are still standing.

Above: School teaching was a profession open to both sexes, especially unmarried women, although teaching did not enjoy high status. This class photograph was taken in 1896 and shows the staff and pupils of McGregor's School, Penicuik. Mr McGregor is standing on the left and next to staff member Miss Black.

Left: Domestic service and housekeeping provided employment for thousands of unmarried women. Jane Rowlegan became housekeeper to the Steuarts of Mount Esk in 1871, when she was twenty-eight years old. She remained with family for thirty-four years.

The joiners' shop at James Tait & Sons, builders at Penicuik, in the early 1900s.

PC Henry Mackenzie and his step-granddaughter Elizabeth at the Old Police Station, Lasswade in 1907. The Midlothian County Police Force was formed in 1840, although police constables were appointed in Dalkeith in the eighteenth century.

Above: Shops and shopping. Staff outside the Newtongrange branch of the Dalkeith Co-operative Society, *c.* 1914. The windows are crammed with attractive displays and advertising.

Left: A brewery had existed in Back Street (now St Andrews Street), Dalkeith since at least 1789. By the late 1880s it was a substantial operation owned by the firm of McLennan & Urquhart. The boy is carrying a large black cat, possibly belonging to the brewery to keep vermin out of the malt. The gable end of the building advertises 'Dalkeith Ale', which was a favourite local drink.

Right: There are plenty of tempting cakes and fancies in the window of the Penicuik Co-operative Society bakers at Clerk Street, Loanhead in the 1920s. The staff, standing left to right, are Jean Munro, Lily Knox, Lizzie Haig and Minnie Rutherford.

Below: Just across the road from the bakers was William Brown's clothiers, Loanhead. Members of staff stand rather jauntily outside the shop, despite the rain.

Shown here at his stables and yard at Church Street, Loanhead, David Sharp was a well-known scrap metal merchant and general dealer.

Opposite above: Margaret Mitchell and her mobile chip van at Glencorse Gala Day in July 1910. The weather was unseasonably cold so she probably had a successful day.

Opposite below: A street bookie outside the Red Lion Pub, Dalkeith in 1934. In the 1930s gambling was widespread but illegal. Here the bookie is writing down the bets or lines in his notebook. His accomplice is probably watching for the police. Dalkeith Burgh Police Court regularly fined offenders up to £10 for 'street betting offences'.

Roslin has a long history of beekeeping. In the late eighteenth century, James Bonner, a celebrated bee master, was resident in the village. He supplied the Edinburgh gentry with honey and wrote two important books on beekeeping. This photograph from the 1920s shows Mr Young of Roslin tending his beehives. His wife ran the popular Craigathrie tea rooms in the village.

Working lives were not all labour and toil. People made friends and had lots of fun. Taken around 1910, the women of the Valleyfield paper mill are ready for their fancy dress ball.

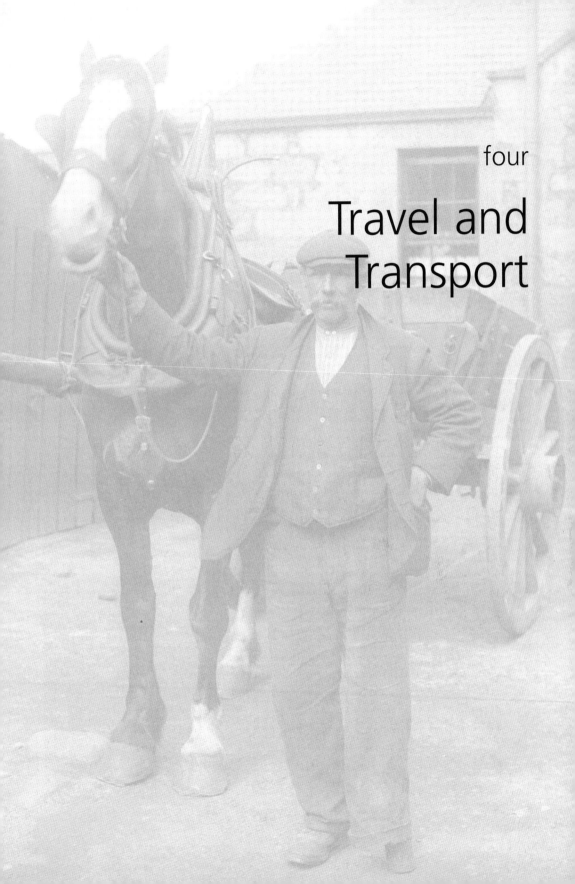

four

Travel and Transport

For centuries, horses were the main method of transport. This charming scene from Roslin Main Street shows a group of ladies outside the post office and a solitary horseman passing by. A small boy crosses the street. There is no danger, pollution or noise in a world before the motorcar.

Christopher Charles Nisbet, a relative of the Steuarts of Mount Esk, proudly displays one of his horses. A solicitor, he is appropriately dressed for country sports.

A horse and trap pass wearily through the village of Temple.

In 1880, William Hunter started business in Loanhead with one horse and cart driving miners to work in Rosewell. By the 1920s, the company had a fleet of vehicles. Here a horse-drawn cart from Hunters is on hire for an outing or a picnic. The horse is beautifully groomed and decorated for the event. Hunter's still run luxury coaches all over the country.

Horses for work. The delivery cart of David Grieve, grocer and provision merchant, Dalkeith.

Horses for pleasure. The ladies of Penicuik Co-operative Society Dressmaking Department and their driver ready for an outing in 1912.

Horses had to be looked after and cared for. Photographed in Roslin, this pipe-smoker is holding a harness and a saddle, and may be the local blacksmith or farrier.

This man is believed to have worked at Slatebarns near Roslin, delivering coal for the Moat pit. At some time, he has clearly lost his left foot or leg, and also possibly his left hand, perhaps as the result of an explosion.

The Howgate Inn near Penicuik opened in 1743. Robert Burns was a regular visitor and Sir Walter Scott is said to have based his character Meg Dods on the inn's landlady Jenny Dods. A daily coach ran from the Howgate Inn to Edinburgh, ten miles away, and it was the first stop on the road from the city to Peebles and further south.

The Stair Arms Hotel near Pathhead was originally a farmhouse but operated as a coaching inn after the construction of the A68 road in the 1830s. When this photograph was taken in 1915, it was a temperance hotel run by a man called Seator. At the rear of the hotel was a piggery, which would not have been popular with guests!

Lothian Bridge crosses the Tyne near Pathhead. It was built between 1827 and 1831 by Thomas Telford to replace the old crossing at Ford. An outstanding example of engineering elegance, its five arches are 80 feet high.

Turnpike roads were main roads on which tolls were levied for their maintenance. Gates or 'turnpikes' were erected every few miles as well as tollhouses where the toll-keeper lived. Toll roads ceased in the late 1870s but many of the houses survive, such as Fallhills tollhouse at an important crossroads near Howgate.

Cycling was a popular craze before the First World War, especially after the invention of the safety bicycle. A party from Mount Esk prepares to set-off for a spin, two of the women are modestly veiled.

THE FORD TO GLENCORSE OLD CHURCH.

This postcard shows an awkward moment for a lady cyclist on the road to Glencorse old church.

Right: Short Spins Around Edinburgh was published in 1897 and provided useful information for cycling trips into the Lothians, including route descriptions, historical facts, lighting-up times and the best picnic spots en route.

Below: Motorbikes were used during the First World War as military vehicles. After the war, as bikes got cheaper, motorcycling became a popular hobby. This Newtongrange man and his partner are seated on a Dunelt motorcycle, which were made in England between 1919 to 1935. They are well wrapped-up for protection against the weather.

Railways were one of the greatest innovations of the Victorian age. The Edinburgh, Loanhead and Roslin branch line was opened in July 1874. It served mines, local businesses and Glencorse barracks. This photograph shows Loanhead station staff sometime after 1895. The stationmaster is second from the right. The poster on the left advertises the 'direct route' to Aberdeen via the Forth and Tay Bridges.

A railway line from Eskbank to Peebles was opened in July 1855. Leadburn station was one of the intermediate stations on the line. In 1864, Leadburn became an important junction with the opening of a branch line to Dolphinton (population about twenty people).

The mighty Glenesk Viaduct or Lothian Bridge at Newtongrange spans the A7 road and the River North Esk. A twenty-three-arch structure, it was constructed in 1847 for the North British Railway to carry the Waverley line from Edinburgh to Hawick. The building on the left is now the Sun Inn, one of Midlothian's favourite watering holes.

Built between 1864 and 1867, the Esk Valley Railway ran from the Esk Valley junction on the Peebles Railway to the village of Polton, the site of several mills. The line passed Lasswade station, on the left of this photograph, and then over the graceful six-arch viaduct and on to Polton.

The 'pug' engine at Esk Mills, *c.* 1900. The chief engineer Mr Frew is standing in front of the driver's cabin. The engine remained in service until the 1960s.

Penicuik railway station and staff in 1905. A branch line of the Eskbank–Peebles railway, the Penicuik line was opened in 1872 and finally closed in March 1967. The old wagon at the front of the photograph was used for storing coal.

Workers from Eskmill paper mill prepare to leave on an excursion from Eskbridge railway station. The station was opened on 1 July 1874 at a cost of £249 0s 6d. It closed during the First World War, but reopened in 1919. In the 1920s it issued 12,000 tickets per year.

This photograph shows horse buses on Roslin Main Street, c. 1900. The open-top bus on the left is probably an Edinburgh Street Tramway bus. The standard bus had seating for twelve inside and fourteen on the roof – the latter was a penny cheaper! On the right is a four-in-hand 'brake'.

All aboard for the Roslin Tour! A Thornycroft charabanc has arrived at its destination in Main Street, Roslin and the driver and conductor, neatly dressed in their SMT uniforms, stop to have their picture taken. Roslin was a popular destination for day-trippers from Edinburgh.

Above: Two charabancs fill up with passengers outside the shops in Newtongrange, *c.* 1931. The Victoria Temperance Bar at the left of the picture was owned by Bugari Quinto and ran as a restaurant serving food and fizzy drinks. The fish market sold both wet fish and fish and chips in the back shop. (Courtesy of Alex Smith)

Opposite below: Photographed in Clerk Street, Loanhead around 1907, this Maudslay double-deck bus is about to make the journey into Edinburgh. The Scottish Motor Transport Co. Ltd introduced the Loanhead–Edinburgh service in September 1906, the company's first route into Midlothian. The local Co-op is on the left.

During the First World War petrol became very scarce and buses were adapted to run on coal gas. The bus in the centre of this photograph has a balloon gas-bag on the roof. Despite technical problems and obvious dangers, the system served its purpose very well, but was discontinued soon after the end of the war. (Courtesy of Alex Smith)

Clerk St. Loanhead.

Transport for the few. In the 1900s, few people could afford motorcars and motoring was the pursuit of the rich. Outside Rosslyn chapel is a chauffeur and his 1913 Siddeley-Deasy 24hp landaulet. He is wearing a heavy overcoat to protect him from the weather, as the driver's seat was not enclosed.

Transport for the many. A steam traction engine on Bonnyrigg Road, Dalkeith takes a remarkable number of passengers on an outing. They are probably workers from Widnell & Stewart, carpet manufacturers.

Transport for the young. Sylvia Steuart of Mount Esk, who was born in April 1894, in her perambulator.

Transport for the old. An invalid bath chair driven by a donkey – an ingenious and novel use of animal power – in Penicuik Road, Roslin.

Left: Transport in trouble. On the evening of 4 October 1919 a lorry that belonged to James Brown & Co., papermakers skidded off the road at the Telford or 'Coach Hole' Bridge at Penicuik and plunged 40 feet into the River North Esk. The driver and a passenger were killed, although a nine-year-old boy had a miraculous escape.

Below: Making the final journey. A horse-drawn funeral carriage followed by mourners in Newtongrange, 1906. This is the funeral of J. Neilson, the bandmaster of the Silver Band.

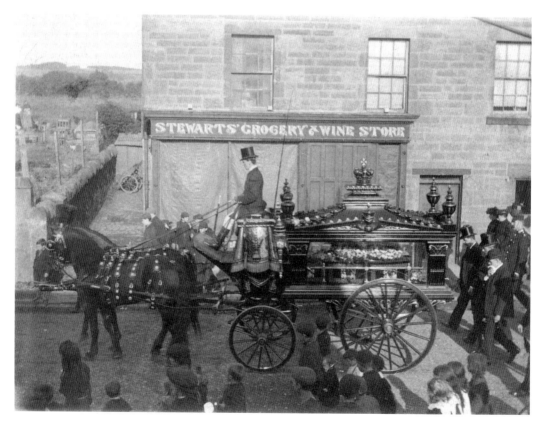

five

Sport and Leisure

Football is the most popular sport in Midlothian with a vibrant non-league and junior scene. This photograph shows the successful Bonnyrigg Rose side of season 1913/14.

The young boys of the Dalkeith Working Lads' Institution side of season 1914/15, with their founder James Tod.

VICTORIA FOOTBALL GROUND, NEWTONGRANGE.

In August 1924, Newtongrange Star Football Club opened a handsome new ground at Victoria Park, the first match being a 5-1 defeat to Raith Rovers.

Rugby football also has its adherents in Midlothian. Here are Penicuik RFC in season 1924/25. The club played its first game in January 1924, losing 33-3 to Lasswade. Back row: K. Ferguson, A. Dickson, A. Noble, A. Spalding, C. Badger, D. Crooks, E. Valence and A. Buchan. Middle: A. Melville, J. Patterson, A. Quinn, R. Graham and J. Cowan. Front: W. Ferrier and J. Audison.

Curling is Scotland's 'roaring game'. Roslin Curling Club was founded in 1816 and in 1895 an artificial pool was created just outside the village. In the bitterly cold winter of 1910-11 conditions were ideal for play.

Bowling became a very popular pastime in the late nineteenth century, both amongst the middle and working classes. Penicuik Bowling Club was instituted in June 1903 after a series of fund-raising events. This photograph shows the opening of the new clubhouse in 1905.

A pastoral setting for the bowling green at Polton. Note the railway signal box in the background.

This postcard shows the opening of Pathhead bowling green on 19 June 1909. The first match was held a few days later when the team of Mr Peter Simpson, the vice-president, defeated that of Mr W. Alexander, the president. (Courtesy of Alex Smith)

1904

GOLF COURSE & VIADUCT, GLENCORSE.

R. R. R.
E

Above: Golfers at Glencorse golf course, which was instituted in 1895, had the challenge of playing over or through the railway viaduct at Milton Bridge. The architect was Robert Bouch, who also built the ill-fated Tay Railway Bridge. Opened in 1877, the viaduct lasted considerably longer than its Dundee counterpart and was demolished in 1987.

Left: On a leisurely afternoon, Christian Steuart and her brother George battle it out at Mount Esk. George is appropriately dressed in his knickerbocker suit.

Anyone for tennis? This photograph was taken around 1892 at the Chamberlain's House at Dalkeith Park. Judging by the clothes, the game would not have been very strenuous. Until the First World War, lawn tennis was a game played only by the wealthier classes.

Public tennis courts in the Welfare Park, Newtongrange, c. 1926. By now, tennis had spread down the social scale. The street behind is Park Road.

The young ladies of Eskbank Girls' School (and a few boys) play cricket in King's Park, Dalkeith in 1909. (Courtesy of Craig Statham)

Eager young lads taking part in a three-legged race at Roslin in June 1902.

A coaching party from Roslin enjoy the fresh air and scenery in the Pentland hills, *c.* 1900.

Roslin Glen has always been a popular picnic spot, as shown in this postcard from 1906.

Opposite above: The reading room at the Newtongrange Miners' Institute, which was opened in 1911. Talking, smoking and spitting were strictly prohibited.

Opposite below: In April 1903, the choir of Loanhead United Free Church Band of Hope gave a successful 'Kinderspiel' production of *Dan the Newsboy* in front of a packed Drill Hall.

Left: Two boys playing in the Loan Burn near Penicuik. (Courtesy of Penicuik Historical Society)

Below: Fishing at Gladhouse Reservoir in the Moorfoot hills. An impressive feat of engineering, the reservoir cost over £63,000 to construct and was opened in 1879 to supply fresh water to Edinburgh.

Gladhouse "The Moorfoots" Reservoir

Left: Founded in 1859, the Volunteer movement was the forerunner of the Territorial Army. The Volunteers provided men with comradeship, training camps and also smart uniforms. This photograph from 1892 shows Penicuik members of the 6th Volunteer Battalion the Royal Scots. Back row: John Arthur, James Gordon and Rob Cockburn. Front row: George Arthur, Andrew Sharp and R.E. Black.

Below: Non-commissioned officers in the Penicuik Volunteers, 1897. Back row: J. Davidson, J. Arthur, W. Arthur, J. Robertson, J. Arthur and J. Smith. Middle row: W. Bell, J. Forsyth, G. Drugger, F. McNulty and A. Robb. Front row: R.E. Black.

Right: Boasting one of the finest beards in the county, Corporal Joe Bailey was a stalwart of the Penicuik Volunteers and also the battalion bugler. On one occasion, he was carrying a basket of provisions for the men when he slipped and fell in the river and was left clinging to the basket, thus earning the nickname 'Moses'.

Below: The last post. Non-commissioned officers of the 6th Volunteer Battalion the Royal Scots photographed on 31 March 1908, the final day of the Volunteers before the introduction of the Territorial Army.

Midlothian has always been a very musical place. Young boys accompany a bagpipe in West Street, Penicuik, *c.* 1910. (Courtesy of Penicuik Historical Society)

Brass bands are one of the great traditions of Midlothian, especially in the mining communities. This photograph shows Bonnyrigg Burgh Band on a trip to Kirkcaldy in 1898.

Christian Stuart of Mount Esk casts an admiring glance at her brother James as he practices his cello. Although disparaging about his abilities, he was good enough to play in orchestras in Edinburgh and London.

THE MAYPOLE, PUBLIC PARK, PENICUIK

Dancing at the maypole in the public park, Penicuik.

Children at play! Boys playing marbles or 'bools' in Penicuik. (Courtesy of Penicuik Historical Society)

Unabashed public bathing in the River North Esk at Sandy Bank, Dalkeith, *c.* 1903. The naked boy later became a Justice of the Peace in Berwickshire! In the background is the sluice gate that served the local iron mill.

Welfare Park in Newtongrange was opened on 11 September 1926 to provide miners and their families with open space for recreation and fresh air. After the opening ceremony, Viscount Chelmsford, chair of the Miners' Welfare Committee, joined three local schoolgirls, who had been instructed to 'look decorative', on the swings.

Welfare Park extended to 17 acres and included a putting green, a pavilion and children's play area with a popular 'shuit'.

Before the invention of television, going to the cinema was a way of life, providing escapism and comfort. The Picture Palace in Newtongrange opened in January 1915 and offered patrons 'Drama, Interest, Latest War Pictures, Comic and Keystone Comedy'. The programme changed four times weekly with three showings on a Saturday, all for 3d admission.

Amateur dramatics have always been a popular way of passing the long winter evenings. The Loanhead Station Ironworks Choir was founded in the 1920s and between 1926 and 1931 they staged a series of successful musical plays, all under the baton of Anthony Docherty, the headmaster of St Margaret's School. A scene from *The Toreador* (1930).

Characters from various productions of the Loanhead Station Ironworks Choir: *Hong Kong* (1928) and *The Country Girl* (1929) (above); and *The Toreador* (1930) and *The Earl and the Girl* (1931) (below).

The Penicuik Boys' Brigade at their annual picnic at Brunstane Castle in June 1898, where they had an 'excellent time' playing games and drilling with wooden rifles. Youth organisations such as the Boys' Brigade and the Scouts were designed to instil in children notions of good behaviour, self-respect and discipline, but they were also about having fun and useful leisure. Sports and summer camps were very popular.

The Loanhead Scouts enjoy life under canvas at their summer camp at Bellanridge near Peebles in July 1926.

six

Days to Remember

Loanhead Children's Gala Day was first held on 22 July 1903, although it had links with older events. Traditionally, the honour of being Gala Day Queen was awarded to the dux of school, the right rotating between the town's three schools. This photograph from 1907 shows Queen Margaret Cairns with her supporters posed on a decorated cart.

Penicuik Children's Gala Day was first held in July 1906. The event had close links with local Friendly Societies. The first Gala Day Queen was chosen in 1914. This photograph from 1931 shows the crowning of Queen Catherine Stewart. The banner in the background is from the Penicuik Oddfellows.

A quartet of Midlothian Gala Day Queens. Above: Joanna Jardine (Loanhead, 1914) and Nan Durie (Penicuik, 1923). *Below:* Lizzie Meek (Newtongrange, 1925) and Mary Affleck (Glencorse, 1926).

Queen Annie Hamilton and her 'gaily attired' supporters, July 1910. Roslin Children's Gala Day started in 1909. The Gala Day Queen was the focus of the day's events.

Roslin Gala Day Queen Mae Young and her supporters in August 1932. After the crowning ceremony, children marched to the local park, headed by the Penicuik Salvation Army Band, where there was an afternoon of sports.

Newtongrange Children's Gala Day was first held in 1913. These photographs were taken at a Gala Day in the late 1920s. Led by a banner, the procession passes rows of miners' cottages (top); the Silver Band in full flow near the Welfare Park (middle); and the procession of the Gala Day Queen in the park (bottom). (Courtesy of Alex Smith)

Left: The Penicuik Hunter Festival began in 1936 and is a modified version of the older Common Ridings that take place in the Scottish Borders. This photograph shows the first Hunter and Lass, Thomson Aikman and Greta Cunningham. The Hunter is wearing a top hat and a scarlet hunting jacket, and both of them are wearing a sash and rosette of office.

Below: In June 1927, the girls of Dalkeith High School and Andrew Somerville, a local baker, won first prize for the best dressed motor at the annual fancy dress parade, which was held in aid of the Dalkeith Children's Gala Day. Runner-up was William Adams, whose butcher's van is grotesquely decorated with a bull and sheep heads and a stuffed pheasant.

Above: Dalkeith Fair was a major annual event.
Workers had a holiday, the travelling 'shows'
arrived and set up on the High Street. Young men
would take their sweethearts to the stalls to try
and win them a souvenir.

Right: Farm labourers came for the Dalkeith
Hiring Fair to find employment for the coming
year. Both of these photographs were taken
around 1934.

Royal visits have always been great occasions in Midlothian. A commemorative arch was built at the west end of Dalkeith High Street to welcome the Prince of Wales (later George V) and Princess Mary in 1907.

Decorations on Gauld the Chemist's shop on Dalkeith High Street for the visit of the Prince of Wales in 1907.

Dalkeith High Street was packed with cheering crowds for the visit of King Edward VII and Queen Alexandra in May 1903.

The 17th Lancers ('The Death or Glory Boys') on the Dalkeith to Gilmerton road in May 1903. The Lancers acted as an escort to King Edward VII, who presented them with war medals at Dalkeith Palace. The local newspaper commented that they made 'an imposing spectacle as they swept up the roadway with their lances glinting in the sunlight'.

The Diamond Jubilee of Queen Victoria in 1897 was celebrated with great enthusiasm all over the country (and the Empire). Towns and villages held various civic events, especially parades and processions. Here on 22 June 1897 children in Loanhead congregate outside the parish church prior to marching around the town. Later, they were presented with gift 'bags' and commemorative mugs.

In August 1904, Indian representatives of the Salvation Army, who had recently attended an International Congress of Salvationists in London, made a short visit to Penicuik. They attended a special missionary meeting in the parish church and visited the local paper factory. Their visit excited great interest, many locals never having seen such exotic people before.

The South African or Boer War (1899-1902) aroused great patriotic fervour and strong passions. This photograph was taken in Peebles Road, Penicuik and shows young boys carrying out pretend drills during the war. The military was held in particularly high esteem at this time and children were encouraged to look up to them.

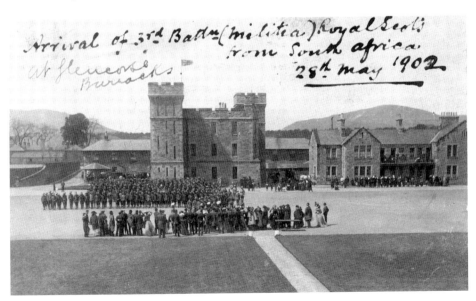

This rare postcard shows the return of the 3rd Battalion the Royal Scots from South Africa on 28 May 1902. The battalion was largely composed of local men, all of whom had volunteered for service overseas. The battalion served for over two years but fortunately sustained only light casualties.

On the evening of Sunday 21 July 1912, the residents of Gorebridge were astonished by the arrival of a 'flying man'. Robert B. Slack was attempting to fly his monoplane around Britain to promote the aviation course at the International Correspondence Schools, London. Flying from Moffat, Slack lost his way and landed to ask directions, but was persuaded to spend the night. He flew away next day after some locals had autographed his plane!

James Crossar Ewart was an eminent zoologist who lived in Craigiebield House, Penicuik. In the late 1890s, he conducted a series of animal breeding experiments, crossbreeding zebras with horses to produce hybrid animals, such as this Young Burchell's zebra with 'shadow stripes'. He published his results in a book called *The Penycuik Experiments* (1899). Midlothian remains at the forefront of animal technology. In the 1990s, the Roslin Institute created the world's first cloned sheep, known affectionately as Dolly.

Above and below: Animal welfare was less important to our predecessors and most people thought little about exploiting animals for entertainment. These remarkable photographs from Penicuik show a travelling showman or gypsy and his dancing bear, which would have performed tricks in return for money. Taken in West Street, the close proximity of the children also shows little regard for safety. (Courtesy of Penicuik Historical Society)

In Scotland, Free Gardeners Societies date back to the seventeenth century. Originally designed to promote and regulate the gardening profession, they evolved into Friendly Societies whose main aim was the mutual benefit and protection of members by providing sickness benefits, pensions, grants and annuities. Penicuik Thistle Lodge was founded in 1822. This photograph was taken in July 1908 and shows lodge officials or 'wardens' with the 'lodge basket', the fine floral display in the centre which was carried in procession, and also the lodge banner.

The Penicuik Free Gardeners held public events to encourage membership and raise their profile, including a formal Gardeners' Walk or Demonstration held annually in summer, as shown here in July 1911. Some of the members carried baskets of flowers and there was a wagon provided for older brethren. After the walk, members took part in a grand dinner and a dance.

The Free Gardeners made ample use of symbolism, including floral tributes and brightly coloured sashes and sceptres for office holders. They were also keen to involve their families in some events. At the Gardeners' Walk in July 1909, girls dressed in white and bearing baskets of flowers represented the Biblical 'ten virgins' and there was also a costumed character called 'Old Adam'.

Midlothian has its share of extreme weather. In September 1891, torrential rain caused severe flooding on the River North Esk. Several bridges were destroyed, including the railway bridge at Kevock. In the background are the woods of Polton House estate and the chimney at Kevock paper mill, which was also affected by flooding.

Heavy snow lying in Roslin High Street, probably April 1908, when snow was recorded as being eight inches deep.

The Penicuik Co-operative Society was founded in July 1860 with forty-eight members. It was very successful and 'Store' branches were opened in other Midlothian towns. On the night of Saturday 6 March 1904, the Co-op's central premises on the High Street were destroyed by fire, causing around £15,000 worth of damage and the loss of many members' passbooks. Adderley's photographic studio was also gutted and a huge number of glass-plate negatives were lost.

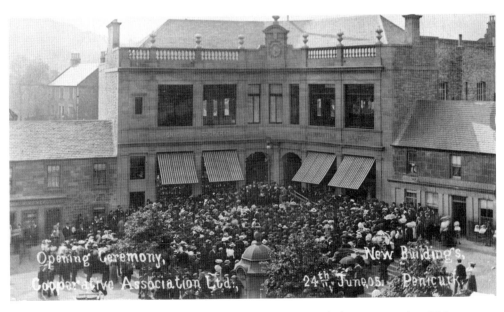

Undeterred, the Co-operative Society quickly rebuilt its premises, which were opened on 24 June 1906. The building had a fine Classical frontage and every modern convenience, including a 'Lamson' pneumatic tube cash system for carrying the money to central accounts.

Work on the new sewerage and purification works on the River North Esk at Penicuik, which were completed in May 1905. There was great civic pride in Victorian and Edwardian Britain and town councils undertook many ambitious projects to enhance the social good. The gentlemen looking on were members of the town council.

On 22 June 1911, to mark the coronation of George V, Provost James Tod of Dalkeith, accompanied by civic dignitaries and a large crowd of onlookers, unveiled an ornamental fountain and electric lamp at Eskbank Toll, an important junction of six roads. (Courtesy of Norman Brett)

The First World War had an enormous impact on communities in Midlothian. On 5 August 1914 the Penicuik Silver Band led the local Territorial regiment, the 16th Royal Scots, away to war. At the front of the soldiers is Major James Tait, who later became Provost of Penicuik. (Courtesy of Penicuik Historical Society)

R.F.A. Signalling School — Dalkeith. July – Oct. 1918

During the war, the grounds at Dalkeith Palace was home to an army signalling school, as shown in this group photograph from late 1918.

During the First World War, the absence of men meant that women were drafted in to do traditional male labour, such as these emergency postwomen photographed in Penicuik in 1917.

Andrew Watson was a typical young man of his generation. He lived in Downie Place, Loanhead with his grandmother and worked at Springfield paper mill. He was a committed Christian, and sang in the church choir and taught at the Sunday school. He enlisted in the 4th Battalion the Royal Scots and was killed in action at Gallipoli on 28 June 1915, aged nineteen. His body was never recovered or identified and he is commemorated on the Helles memorial, Turkey. (Courtesy of Norman Brett)

The declaration of peace was celebrated in Penicuik on 19 July 1919. Amongst other events was an official welcome for 'returned heroes' and a fancy dress parade for children. This photograph shows the 'Allied Nations Car' with local schoolgirls dressed to represent the victorious allies.

Penicuik war memorial was unveiled on Sunday 8 May 1921. A St Martin's cross of grey granite, the bronze panels bear the names of 171 local men who lost their lives in the war.

Other local titles published by Tempus

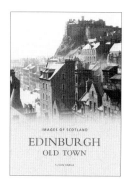

Edinburgh Old Town

SUSAN VARGA

In this beautiful collection of 200 images from the Edinburgh Room of the Central Library, Susan Varga presents a pictorial history of Edinburgh's Old Town. The images cover the area known as the Royal Mile and include Castlehill, the Lawnmarket, High Street, Canongate, Grassmarket and George IV Bridge as well as the royal residences of Holyroodhouse and Edinburgh Castle. The Old Town underwent regeneration during the twentieth century and it has now developed into a centre of tourism and a site of World Heritage importance.

0-7524-4083-7

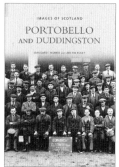

Portobello and Duddingston

MARGARET MUNRO AND ARCHIE FOLEY

This fascinating collection of over 200 images provides a pictorial history of Portobello, famous as a seaside holiday resort, and the adjoining parish of Duddingston, which still maintains its rural village life centred around the church and the loch. The images reflect the importance of both the tourist trade – attracted by the sands, swimming pool and funfairs – and of industry, such as pottery and the manufacture of glass bottles.

0-7524-3657-0

Scotland's Common Ridings

KENNETH R. BOGLE

The Common Riding, Lanimer Day or Riding the Marches, when men ride out to mark the common lands of the burghs, has been an integral part of town and burgh life for much of Lowland Scotland. In the sixteenth century, ridings took place in Edinburgh, Glasgow, Aberdeen, Stirling and Dundee. Today, only a few towns outside the Borders continue to hold ridings. Kenneth Bogle introduces us to the tradition, its histories and the events as they have changed over the years.

0-7524-2992-2

Hibernian Football Club 1875-1975

PAUL LUNNEY

Many of Scotland's greatest post-war footballers have played in the famous green-and-white shirt of Hibernian FC. The 'Famous Five' that tormented defences in Scotland in the late 1940s and early 1950s have since been joined by many other stars who have left their mark at Easter Road. In this comprehensive study of every Hibs player since 1946, there are many stories to be told, including legendary names such as Joe Baker, Franck Sauzee and Pat Stanton.

0-7524-2170-0

If you are interested in purchasing other books published by Tempus, or in case you have difficulty finding any Tempus books in your local bookshop, you can also place orders directly through our website

www.tempus-publishing.com